GIBBONS, THE SINGING APES

Susan Ring

Contents

Rigby
A Harcourt Achieve Imprint

www.Rigby.com
1-800-531-5015

Meet the Gibbons

Imagine that you are walking quietly
through a rain forest. Listen.
You hear a strange, loud song. Look up!
What is that animal singing in the trees?

It's a gibbon!
Gibbons are the smallest animals
in the ape family.
They live in rain forests in the tops
of very tall trees.

Gibbons seem to fly through the trees.
They can jump 20 feet in one leap.
They can move through the trees
at 35 miles an hour!

How do gibbons move through the trees so fast?
They use their long arms and fingers to swing
from tree limb to tree limb.
Their arms are even longer than their legs!

How Gibbons Grow

Look high up in the treetops again.
A baby gibbon is holding on to its mother.
How do baby gibbons grow up in the trees?

The mother gibbon has one baby at a time.
The baby is born without any fur
except on its head.

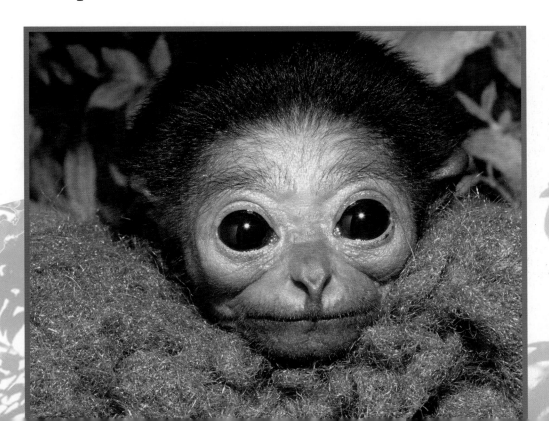

Soon after it is born,
the baby gibbon can
hold on to its mother.
The baby gibbon rides
with its mother
wherever she goes.

A baby gibbon clings to
its mother until it can
take care of itself.
This happens when
the gibbon is about
two or three years old.
The gibbon is an
adult at about six
years old.

Gibbon Families

Gibbons have close families.
The mother and father stay together
all their lives.
The children often stay with their parents
for seven years or more.
Then they leave to start their own families.

The mother is the head of the gibbon family.
She leads everyone through the trees.
She knows where to find the best food.

Gibbon families sleep high
in the tree branches.
Babies hold on to their mothers.
Young gibbons might sleep
in their fathers' arms.

Singing Apes

It's morning in the forest. Listen.
The gibbons have started to sing.
Their song is very loud!

Why do gibbons sing?
They sing to tell other apes
that this part of the forest
is their home.
That is why gibbons are
called the singing apes!

Index